Gilding The Lily

Don Gutteridge

Gilding the Lily

New Poems: 2023

Don Gutteridge

First Edition

Wet Ink Books
www.WetInkBooks.com
WetInkBooks@gmail.com

Gilding the Lily
by Don Gutteridge

Cover Design – Richard M. Grove
Layout and Design – Richard M. Grove
Cover Image – Courtesy of Shutterstock, used by permission.

Typeset in Garamond
Printed and bound in Canada
Printed and Distributed in USA by Ingram,
        – to set up an account – 1-800-937-0152

Library and Archives Canada Cataloguing in Publication

Title: Gilding the lily : new poems, 2023 / Don Gutteridge.
Names: Gutteridge, Don, 1937- author.
Identifiers: Canadiana 20230585655 | ISBN 9781998324002 (softcover)
Subjects: LCGFT: Poetry.
Classification: LCC PS8513.U85 G55 2023 | DDC C811/.54—dc23

Table of Contents

Five more for Tom

First Impressions
Early Days with Anne

Addendum

The poems in this section were penned after the publication of *First Impressions: Early Days with Anne* (First Choice Books: 2023)
These too are dedicated to Anne who made love her gift to the world.

Let Love In

Autumn 1960

I don't recall the number
of times I fell in love
(or out of it), but I must've
been all of ten when Nancy
swam into my cunning ken,
who made my heart flutter
like a hummingbird in heat,
or Shirley, the girl-next-door
whose durable curves stirred
something well below
my tantalized ticker, or Marybelle
Cooper with the bedroom eyes
I longed to loop in mine,
or Laura, whose skin-thin
jeans varnished her vee,
and O my four fraught
years at Western's U,
where no lithesome lass
disturbed my celibate state,
and thus, when you swept into
view, all your girlish
gimmickry gone, freckle-
friendly and easy to know,
there was no more need
for pinup Nancys or gorgeous
Lauras: I simply returned
your smile, and let love in.

Gilding the Lily

Whenever I praise your paintings
or remark on their artful "bleeds"
and "blues," or commend the myriad
ways your brush utters
its dainty daubs, you give me
the gaze that says, "No need
to gild *this* lily."

Matron

Preston: Autumn 1960

You take me to meet your best
friend's mother, the formidable
Missus D., an aproned
matron who knows her own
mind and any other
within reach of its claws,
and she peers at me over
her pince-nez like a punter
appraising the favourite or a suitor
totting up the widow's worth,
and pauses long enough
to give you a sideways glance
that says, "He'll do."

Other Loves

Preston: Autumn 1960

You take me to a party
in a friend's rec room
and introduce me to Fritz,
the Preston lad you paled
around with before you took on
Toronto and its citied glitz,
wheeling your father's dusty
pickup about town
like the Lone Ranger and Tonto
on a toot, and I imagine
your unalloyed laughter
when he guns the gas or lays
rubber, his darling arm
giving yours a teasing squeeze,
and what relief to find him
now well-wived, and know
we've both born the bloom
of other loves, and survived.

Breaking Bread

Autumn: 1960

On our daily commute to school
and back, at five each day
we stop to nosh at the Swisse
bistro with the quaint Tyrolean
scrolling and, your own
repast yet to come,
you watch me, with disinterested
delight, as I feast upon
porterhouse, still bleeding,
festooned with mushrooms
and sauteed onions, wondering
perhaps with your gastronomic
eye whether I have room
for a second feed or the apple
pie.

Teeming

Autumn: 1960

I loved the voluptuous vim
of your Volks and the way you gunned it
whenever it misbehaved
like an Indie winner goosing
the juice, and me beside you
in the wombed cocoon of the car
with the windows down, the cinnamon
hues of your hair abloom
in the breeze, and when you let
the fingers of your free hand
flutter from the wheel and take
the measure of mine, I want
to rave like some demon
lover, teeming with words
he cannot utter.

Uncle (*by marriage*)

You tell me about your uncle
Bram, who watercoloured
local landscapes and, thinking
he might be Van Gogh rejigged,
bobbed his locks, nursed
a Van Dyke, and passed his genius
along to a prepubescent
pupil, who dreamed of pushing
a perambulator with a baby
Bram tucked inside,
but as luck would have it, the would-be
Breugel got two years
less a day for corrupting a minor,
and you his last gouache,
which we have to admit is almost
good.

Wink

Autumn 1960

Odd, isn't it? I never
called you 'my girl;'
as if I'd wooed and won you
(as much as I'd hoped for a
dream romance, showing you off
on my amiable arm like first
prize in some Kinsmen's raffle),
but even so, you kept
something of the girl curled
inside like a filigreed fern,
and let it grow where it would,
and I see it by chance in the
sideways swerve of your smile
or the light that bedizens your eyes
whenever you give me a wink
or a nod.

Toddle

Autumn 1960

Love was the last thing
on my mind when you took me
under your welcoming wing
and toddled me off to sin
city, for I was still
smarting from half-a-dozen
amorous escapades that ganged
agley, and there was nothing
predatory in the blue illume
of your eyes or the freckled fringe
of your smile, and I don't remember
when, but something akin
to love or its cousin wobbled
my toddle and waylaid my heart.

A-Flat

December 1960

O how you loved your music!
Friday nights in the student
pews of Massey Hall,
humming along with Brahms
or Beethoven, or sighing aloft
to Tosca's dying diminuendo,
and it was you who introduced me
to Ella and Leadbelly's basso
bravura, and when you take me
to a housewarming party
and the room erupts in sentimental
song, and I add my whiskey-
whetted tenor to the mix,
your own wee voice pipes up
beside me, and I catch in your musical
chatter a sharp that oughta-be
flat, and realize that the girl
I'm over-the-moon-about
     can't carry a tune

Where it Would

December-January:1960-61
For Anne in fond memory

When I finally got up enough
nerve to give you a kiss
with full-lipped zip
and our tongues tangled in twinned
vim, you happened to mention
you weren't a fan of animate
osculation, and so thereafter
we nibbled lobes or nudged
noses (like fur-blurred Innuit
keeping their igloo juiced)
or hugged like siblings at a
family fête, letting
love bloom where it would
in the parked dark.

Orthodox

Christmas week: 1960

I wasn't sure whether you
were the kind of gal who welcomed
roses or chocolates in a
beribboned box, but then
again, those smitten
have never been keen on the
petty protocols of courting
or the palpitating pages of
True Romance, but taking
no chances and tethering
my wits, I eschewed the orthodox
red, and chose instead
a dozen long-stemmed
yellows, hoping they'd find you
one of the "whethers," and let
her know we were more than pals.

Abuzz

Christmas 1960

Come Christmas, we spend
our first days apart
since the daily commutes to school
began, and already I miss
the vellum of your voice and the way
you smile quietly with your eyes,
and when the note arrives
like a lover's billet-doux
thanking me for the roses
that spoke the flurried words
I'd yet to say aloud,
something in my heated heart
went abuzz, letting it know
that this is what love does.

Gibbous

January, 1961

There may've been a gibbous
moon as we cuddled in the velvet
velour of your Volks, but I was
looking elsewhere for light,
and found it in the living lustre
of your glance, in the shine your eyes
used to surprise the world
and lend it your loveliness,
and when our lips met
in blissful collusion, and browsed
a while, I felt the new-moon
glow that only love allows.

In the Heart

February, 1961

I might've said 'I love you'
the night of my rose-wrapt
proposal; I must have done
because I'd rehearsed it like a
distracted actor, frightened
of the stage, but as I recall
you didn't return the favour
(your answer lay in the amorous
ambit of your glance), but in the
long years of our parallel,
caring lives, those love-
laden words remained,
in whole or part, were they mattered
most: in the heart.

A Very Modern Woman

June 1961

Although you are a modern
woman in every way,
comfortable in the skin you've been
given, sure of the skills
you've learned to wield in the
cut-and-thrust of the classroom,
or bent lovely above
your *Singer* that plays whatever
tune you tootle, or when
you persuade your awkward, ungainly
charges to give their luck
a try with a purring pot or
subtle soufflé – you wear white
at the wedding, wrapped in satin
like a swathed goddess, a tiara
tucked in the ginger tingle
of your hair, and you may've been
anybody's everyday bride,
but come rain or conjugal shine,
you are mine.

At Home

Autumn: 1961

I was puzzled at first when you failed
to remark, as compliment or query,
upon the latest outburst
of my poetic art, cunningly
placed where even a blind
Philistine might find it and be tempted
to take its temperature, but then
I recalled that you had not
played host to a poem or the reach
of its rhyme since Grade 12,
when a D-Day vet, sweating
to get the rhythm right,
stumbled on the tum-ta-tum
of the Bard's pentameter and added
a syllable to the great man's
name, but I took notice
of the glow in your eyes whenever
they found a painting to prize,
or the buzz you got when steeped
in the stories of Laurence or Munro,
and I knew that somewhere inside
there'd be, one day, a home
for my poems, and me.

Haberdashed

You don't invite me to tag
along when you pick out
your wedding dress: a simple
satin, wimple-white,
uncluttered by lace
or furbelow, but yours is all
the beauty it needs to glow
on the morning we are wed,
and in the lustrous luft
of your locks: a diadem,
that might've graced the brow
of the Faeiry Queen, or garlanded
Guin, and though I'm no
handsome Lance in my borrowed
blazer and baggy pants,
we make a perfect nuptial
couple, haberdashed by love.

Truly Wed

June 30, 1961

There was no confetti to garnish
the egress of the happy couple,
and the reception was held in the
Legion Hall among portraits
of mustachioed generals and bracketed
plaques of battles no longer
remembered, and your mother carried on
with her principled boycott of all
things conjugal or wedding-
blessed, and the father of the bride
looked on with benign regard,
and footed the bill, and my mother
still wondered which twin
did the wooing, and my brother kept
his wonderings wrapped, and we noshed
on indifferent chicken and warm
wine, and no one thought
to offer a toast to your loveliness,
or rise to give the groom
tips on his bedroom etiquette,
but whatever the dos and don'ts
of the day, and after all
was done and said, we were truly
wed.

Tendrils

June 30, 1961

I come to the marriage bed
with my macho's apparatus intact,
but lacking a practice run,
you, however, wise
in the ways of womanhood
and the world, bid me lie
beside your beckoning beauty
with the ease of a chatelaine
offering tea and sympathy,
and so it was: our maiden
conjugal clutch was softened
and made mavellous by the
gentled tendrils of your touch.

c

Elora: Autum 1961

The Drew domicile, where we camped
for a teaching-year was Tory-
blue from the footings up,
until the Denholm clan
hued it Liberal-red,
and when the writ was dropped
that Autumn, we decided to give
the new team, like Tommy's
troupe, a try (you'd always
rooted for the little guy
and the flawed logic of lost
causes), and so it was
that we planted an NDP
banner in the pampered grass
of George's storied chateau,
and let its green sheen
shine.

Carrying On

Elora: September 1961

In the autumn after the wedding,
we took up housekeeping
in the servants' quarters of the George
Drew family homestead
like proper (if paupered) patricians,
basking in the reflected glow
of that old-school Tory,
and on our first night therein,
in the midst of an overly
enthusiastic bout of communing,
the bed collapsed under us,
and when we stopped laughing
and the mattress proved doable,
we carried on communing.

The Best

Autumn: 1962

Thinking to master something
other than my tantrums, I elect
to become an academic, lean
on a lectern and profess, my briar
smouldering in a freshly threshed
beard, and so, we pull up
stakes: *you* giving up
your Home Ec and *I*
the job that paid the bills,
and Autumn finds *me*
at Western U and *us*
in a cramped flat you make
livable with a dash of paint
where it matters and a love-seat
you resuscitate and wrap in blue-
hued bunting, and curtains
confected out of superannuated
sheets, and if home is where
the heart is, I confess: this
is the one that beats best.

Coach

I sit in the kitchen, a room
apart, its door ajar,
and listen as you persuade
a six-year-old dyslexic
to read, and when he (it's always
a he) feels his tongue
stumble on a stubborn syllable,
you feed him the word and the next,
if needed, to keep the coached
flow going, and I hear
the joy in his voice at making
sense at last of alphabetic
conundrums, and knowing, as a rookie
reader, the glow that comes
with the whole story and the ginger
cookie that follows.

Booster

You never mentioned whether
or not you'd read a poem
of mine from the many books
that bulged on my shelves and begged
attention, and when for a time
you came to the public readings
I gave like a starved parson
in his poetry pulpit, I thought
perhaps that might've been you
applauding like an enthused booster,
or some claque the wily bard
had planted in the back row —
even so, I took your silence
as consent, secretly pleased
not to be asked what a gnarly
line implied or a metaphor
meant, happy to have someone
like you at myside, letting her laureate
crow, like a rooster in love
with his lot.

If I were the Bard

(a sort of sonnet)

If I were the Bard of Avon
I should compare thee to a summer's day
and sing you a goodly sonnet
with a closing couplet that rhymes
with love or roses, but my bourgeoning
verse bubbles up from no
Pierian Spring, nor does it dance
to a faux-Shakespearean tune,
but I'd bring down the moon
and the harbouring stars and put them
in a poem of my own making
that plumbs your loveliness and brims
your beauty, and leaves no trace
of Arden's bard or a summer's day.

Honey Dew

With a nod to the Bard

How like thou art to a
summer's morn, when sunshine
gilds the pastured grasses
and sets the leaves alight
and teasing breezes splay
and knit, and so you:
your beauty born anew
each dawning day,
your love, wakening to the world's
wit and me, like the honey
dew on June's reposing
roses.

Ginger

No-one thought to call you
cute when you were just
a toddler with carotene curls
that wandered where they will
and a forest full of freckles,
but then, they failed to notice
the jewelled blue beauty
of your eyes, the selfsame gaze
that kickstarted my heart,
took my breath away
and gave it back renewed,
with a ginger fringe and a peck
of freckles thrown in
for good measure.

Urgent

My village was an upright
little town, where the girls,
though willing, didn't, and the guys
could, but wouldn't, and if,
by chance, a romance got
too raunchy, a shotgun
wedding kept it licit,
but just below this wobbling
façade lay a seething sea
of priapic bachelors and urgent
virgins.

Nuggeting

I might've turned just ten
when I first observed that the grade-
eight girls, bouncing
ball and double-Dutching
in their own untroubled yard,
had curves where I did not,
and curls the breeze busied
before it whirled their skirts
awry, but we were too shy
to animadvert, happy
enough with the lot we'd got
because the nuggeting of lust
had yet to pounce.

Five more for Tom

In fond memory

Flawed

Ahh, Tom, you were such a
cherub-cheeked, blue-
eyed babe with a mop
of ginger curls on top
(like an angel not yet estranged
from the flock) that I wanted
to stop the clock where it stood
and tuck you somewhere safe
from Time's tyrannical touch,
like a scarab, amplified in amber,
and find you there each morning
in your toddler's crib, a-gaze
at the world as if its days
were not the doings of a flawed
God.

Sliver

I promised you that I'd given up
weeping at your lonely going,
but still, some sentimental
sliver of song, held too long
in the heart, can set the tears
a-teem and catch my breath
abaft, letting me know
that Love is more durable
than Death, and dapples the dreams
that keep it living.

The Eyes Don't Lie

Gibbons Park: 1988

You might've been three
when you first played peekaboo
between the towering trunks
of weathered willows in Gibbons
and I snapped this photo for my pleasure
and posterity: your ginger curls
doing their best not to curdle
or fling themselves free,
and the poseur's look you give me
and the lens is a sort of impish
grin in a Frankenstein frown:
all teeth and pinched
squint, but the eyes don't lie,
the love they carried, ablaze
from birth, tarries there,
and I would give the Earth
my bones to bury for one
last peek at their loving
gaze.

Rain-Honed Roses

Three years almost since you've
been gone, and the shock of your loss
still stings like a bee in the brain,
and each Spring that comes
and goes with its perfect green
promise lets me know
you are not here to see
the lilacs bud and bloom
again or rain-honed
roses rupture red,
and I must face the terrible
beauty of Being – alone.

Only Begotten

How often, when, at the loss
of one I loved, have I wished
I could believe that the "soul"
was anything other than the zeitgeist
of the living, or that God so loved
the world He gave His only
begotten to set our souls
free from the body's burdening
ballast and let them float
in the leavening halls of Heaven,
or that some semblance of what
we were or hoped to be,
other than the ripple of remembrance,
outlasted the failing of the flesh –
but you have gone to your grave
and taken your "soul" with you,
and O how I'd like to whisper
in your happily heathen ear:
"Jesus saves!"

His Nibs

For Bruce Ashdown in fond memory

You set your sails so close
to the wind, your cunning craft
wobbled on the waves like a
lopsided lobster, and came about
with such surprise your lucky
duck was just enough
to keep your head from severing,
but you always had steady hand
on the tiller, at sea or otherwise,
and when the wind turned whimsical,
you hoisted your spinnaker like a
lunatic balloon, and bid
your jib work its will
on the bobbin of the breeze.

The Nod

When the Sunday sun is warm
enough to bring the honey
bees buzzing from the hive
to nosh on the nectar of a dozen
cousin flowers, and lolling
swallows swoon before they swarm
in the butterfly-fluttering breeze,
and dew-worms uprise
to sip the misted morsels
of the morning, the world is Sabbath-
fabulous, waiting for a God
to give it the nod.

Howl

When I first heard that our dear
neighbour, John McCleiister,
had had a heart attack and died,
I pictured some prowler with menace
on his mind surprising him in bed
and doing him in then and there,
and when my Gran explained
that he was no longer breathing
and nothing could bring it back,
I realized that, fair or foul,
none of us lives as long as
he likes, no matter how loudly
we howl.

Sparrow

A song sparrow, perhaps,
(my best guess): spotted
breast, yellow bill,
copper cap, settles
on my sitting-room sill,
feathers ruffled like a flustered
fan dancer, looking
to impress, the fresh day
a-leap in its eye, and opens
its beak as if to sing me
something that might salvage
our morning, but no note,
narrow or steep, comes
to comfort or arouse, just
a tree sparrow's fleeting
cheep! cheep!

The Good Indian

Whenever we played cowboys
and Indians, I opted always
to be the Good Indian,
eagle-feathered in doeskin
britches and saliva-softened
moccasins to let me feel
the give of the ground and the ease
of running above it, and I
would sit in the wigwam warmth
and smoke the pipe of peace
among my bronze brothers,
like Jimmy in *Broken Arrow,*
and powwow till my tongue numbed,
and thump on my tom-tom's
tympani like the delirium-dance
of Powassan's drum.

Abrupt

For Effie Free in fond memory
Point Edward: 1945

When wee Effie Free
lay sprawled upon the pavement
like a doll somebody forgot
to love, her morning scoot
for ice cream roughly
abrupted, her father, Ross,
was the unwitting witness,
who took up the drink again,
and thereafter, whenever I passed him
on the street, I was afraid to look him
in the eye, for fear of seeing
the impossible pain, rooted
there.

Whistling Dixie

For John on his 60th

You've just made sixty
without a hair on your head
greying, or gone, and all
your wits still willing,
and in your blue-eyed wake
you've left us a duo of daughters
whose beauty shines from the bloom
of their eyes, and though you're clever
as clever and no-one wishes
to be sixty forever, you've got
a year to keep your class-
act going, and it's only
a thought, but this is a day
to celebrate yourself, and that
ain't whistling "Dixie."

A Mated Pair

A pair of mated hawks
(I think, from the way their wings
waver as one), their eyes
fixed upon the grasses
below, where a pair of mated
mice (I infer, from the way
their whiskers weave as one)
fail to notice the shiver
of shadow that keeps the sun
from their worried scurry, and when
this day is done, the taloned
pair hang eddyless
on the air, sated with mic —
no longer mated.

I Go Public

London, Ontario: October 1962

I was all of twenty-five
and very much full of myself
when I went public with my poems,
sharing the limelight (as it were)
with a pair of bright-eyed
poetesses, one of whom read
with enthusiastic alacrity
and the other in slow, intoning
syllables, mistaking her ponderous
pace for depth or devotion,
and when the applause for them,
pointedly polite, came
to a close with a single, haphazard
clap, I strode to the stage
(a two-inch riser, borrowed
from the nearby *Grand*), like an
Old Testament prophet, come
to deliver the goods from God,
and declaimed the dreadful lines
of my apprentice pieces, about
Brébeuf and his brethren, who martyred
heartily and Sieur de La Salle,
stalking the mosquito-bitten
woods because he could, and Hudson
et fils, who mistook the Beaufort
for a Chinese sea, and when
I'd finally run out of poetic
petrol, the audience, numbed
by the fumes, applauded like encouraging
claques, hoping the bloom
was off my rose.

At Bay

My Gran had a saying or pithy
quip for every occasion,
and if it wasn't "a stitch in time"
or "praise be the Lord," it was
"That'll be a frosty Friday"
or "a watched pot," tossed off
whenever a quick-lipped
sally suited, and I wondered
whether this was her way
of keeping a worm-burled
world at bay.

The Better Bits

For Art Fidler

You follow the daily doings
of my courtship with Anne,
the ups and downs of our pre-
nuptial carousing, like a
fan of *True Confessions*
or a 'blue' bodice-ripper,
making the odd comment
when one was due or not,
urging me on to the better
bits and racy riffs
in the plot, concluding your doctoral
dissertation with, "You two
were quite a pair," and no-one
has summed us up with such
bravura or bite.

Rapture

For Grace Leckie in fond memory

I pride myself on knowing
what urges the birds and the bees,
and what's what in the wider
world, like the do's and don'ts
of 'blue' taboos, but when
Gracie invites me to watch
her roan stallion mount
the piebald mare, we are taken
aback at the blundering shudders
that shiver the rivets in the roof,
and that night I dream of lewd
oozings and losing myself
in rapturous rut.

Ribald

I might've been thirteen, no more,
when the sight of a girlish curl,
napping on a nape, or the telltale
swell of a buttoned blouse
aroused in me feelings
that growled in the groin and stiffened
my resolve, and when I took it
to task, it bloomed a bright
surprise, and reprised that happy
dabble in the dreams I bore
thereafter of a rabbit, ribald
in rut.

Ululation

I don't remember when
(or if anyone told me how)
I learned to ululate
ollie, ollie, en frei
and send my fellow felons
back to the hovering dark
beyond the ambered ambit
of Mara's lamp, but I let it
roll off my Tarzan's tongue
as if it were some coded
scroll from Mars or a chanting
incantation to the
incorruptible country
of the young.

A-Wooing

The girls are doing cartwheels
on the lawn, flashing their panties
and the thews of their thighs, head-
over-heels in elongated loops,
in love with the feel their bodies
bode and something that flutters
its fury where the belly abides,
while the boys look on with side-
ways lurks at such a candid-
carnal display, and wonder
whether the growl in their groin
can be uttered again as words
of wooing.

Cops and Robbers

For John, and for Frankie and Bobby Pepers
London, Ontario: circa 1972

Through the picture window,
 I watch as you and the Pepers
boys, across the road,
are playing cops and robbers,
fretting to and fro
like mad marionettes
with stricken strings and a drunk
puppeteer, and Frankie, who wields
his cap pistol like the Durango
Kid in a six-gun shootout,
pours 'lead' into brother Bob,
who refuses to go down or die,
and during the brouhaha that ensues,
you oblige the game by doing so
yourself with melodramatic antics
and a dying 'sigh' that rattles
the glass I'm looking through,
wondering how great it must be
to be young enough to ululate
your joy, as if nothing else
would do.

Incursions

S.S. No.12: Sarnia TWP.

In the schoolyard at noon
we play endless incursions
of Prisoner's Base, and I am
the first of the crewcut crew
to go zigzagging thru the enemy's
curlicue camp like a rabbit
with a beagle on his butt, flinging
skirts and girls askew,
and making them captives with the
prurient poke of a thumb
or a pat on the bum that jiggles
their giggles, and O how I loved
to be the last man standing
and make my manly dash
thru flustered frocks and pulsing
petticoats, and set free
the better gender to be
whatever God meant
when he made them.

Prize

In Hendrie's stooped coop,
Jo-Anne flashes us
full-frontal, and we are
hypnotized by a brace of
stiffened nipples, atop
twinned breasts as pleasing
as pint-sized pumpkins,
and when her pants drop
vertical, we are like studs
in rut, eyes on the prize
where her whatsit lies.

Doing My Bit

If commandos strike at dawn,
I want to be there when the morning
light quickens their courage,
and in this long-ago photo,
I am heroically helmeted
with toy Tommy-gun aboard,
me: not yet five and the War
still raging somewhere
beyond my ken, where the real
father I'd yet to meet
was making me proud, and though
my gun's a Christmas gift
and my helmet's pith, I feel
as if I'm doing my bit.

Come July

Come July, my world is pied,
where dandelions dot the lawn
like gilded doubloons strewn
on the ocean floor before
they balloon in tufted puffs
and vanish, and daisies
in their sun-fed meadow
are gingham-gay, and shadows
tossed by the big, umbrella'd
elm are checkerboard
chiaroscuro, and the bridal
bouquet on the sill blooms
in petti point profusion,
but all things green
and vegetable-variable succumb
at last to the sampling whims
of the singular, and die.

Hopalong

When Hoppy was done dealing
with the black-vested villains,
stinging their pistoled fists
from ten paces and giving
his guns a celebratory twirl,
the scene shifted to his side-
kick, Lucky, charming
the school marm in her calico
frock, and when he finds
gumption enough to buss
her lickable lips, the boys
in the back row and beyond,
let out a universal, hooting
hiss, and the girls, if there were any,
just smiled, and thought:
"Wait a while."

On the Prowl

For Joanne Hendrie in fond memory

When Joanne began to dance
 in the Hendries' henhouse
that summer when the sun turned
sultry, like a hula-hula
girl, eager to show us
her gender's jewel, and offed
her undies, the jaws of the boistering
blokes dropped further,
but when she called for equal
pay, we hummed and hawed
and jiggled our jaunties till they crooned
like a Hurdy Gurdy on coke
or a punter on the prowl.

Novice

September 1960

As a novice pedagogue, I was braced
for the possibility of the class
cut-up or the smart remark
delivered *sotto voce*
or the gum-chewing hooligan
or the too-pretty girl
in the front row, batting
her lacquered lashes or the
finger-snapping teacher's
pet or the flunked hunk,
big enough to buy
his own booze, sleeping
it off in a window seat
or the hiccupping snicker
at the Bard's anatomical
lapses, but, when Lear
stepped out on the Festival
stage with a dead daughter
a-lie in his arms, howling
down the moon and my stunned
students, I wasn't prepared
for the flutter of their tender, teenage
tears.

All things Botanic

It was Mister Block, who taught us
all things botanic
and zoological, who took me
aside one day and read me
the riot act, insisting
I widen my academic
diet to include a college
degree, and "What's more,"
he adumbrated, "If you don't,
you'll end up flogging vacuums
door-to-door," and I replied,
"I'll give it a try."

Innings

Having had no hands-on
experience to guide my gauche
gallantry in the osculation
game, I was taken aback
when the girl, whose name might've
begun with a "b" skidded
across the seat between us
and en-latched my lower lip,
and when I next took breath
it was a lungful of tongue
that torqued and clung, and I
never knew until then
that the less-vexed sex
had a hunger as randied as my own,
and in the kissing innings
were the oscular boss.

Duck

In the Point when I was young
enough not to be noticed,
you were no-one essential
until you were nicknamed
by a rustic cousin, an unctuous
uncle or an antiquated aunt,
and these mildly mocking
monickers were worn like baptismal
badges, and I so wished
to be labeled, with a wink and a
neighbourly nod, "Shorty"
or "Slim" or a pint-sized
"Pete," but, as luck would have it,
nobody obliged except
a winsome kinsman, who dubbed me
"Duck" – and it stuck.

Tea Dance

Chatham Collegiate Institute: 1955

We called it a tea dance,
but no beverage, innocuous
or not, was ever offered
and the only dancing done
between the gender-generated
rows of boys studying
the flaws in the floor and girls
doing their best to keep
their smiles from drooping
were a tired couple of teachers
trying to adapt the fox-
trot to the painful strains
of "Heartbreak Hotel,"
but something in the music,
however inharmonious,
moved the room to begin:
a shy shuffle or the tap
of a toe or a hum in the blood,
but once begun, the genders
blended, letting go,
losing their all in the
daft delirium of the dance.

License

When a poem comes my way,
I want it to send me reeling
like a punch-drunk pugilist
with too many blows below
the belt, and I want each syllable
to wallow in the welter of its word
before it sings its say,
and when I'm done with bardic
devices and the feelings they flay
and heal, I'll salute my muse
in the higher echelons of Heaven
and thank her for the liar's license.

Rabbit Stew

For my Uncle Potsy in fond memory

I was pleased when my uncle let me
tag along on his afternoon
rabbit shoot, and I watched
in awe as he slung the double-
barreled twelve-gauge
gun over his arm
with the ease of a waiter
three-fingering a tray,
and my role was to jump
on every twigged bundle
of brush we met in hopes
of spooking our prey, and when
at last he came zig-
zagging in panicked disarray,
my uncle let go with both
barrels, and the Easter bunny
we found feigning sleep
in the grass, lay with his eyes
squeezed tight, as if
he'd already seen too much
of the world and its ado,
and welcomed the thought of warm
broth and rabbit stew.

Mercy Match

Edward Street School
Point Edward, 1946

In the shaded coign behind
the school, where I could play
unafraid, free from the big-
bulked bullies prowling
for prey, it was ever aggies
and allies, taws and cat's-eyes,
whenever we could gouge a pot
out of the cindered grit
and someone half my size,
parading on our private patch,
invites me to join him
in a mercy match.

Specimens

The reason roses have no thorns
is simple: to give fair warning
to impetuous pluckers
and because anything with dimples
and seductively garbed must
come to us barbed.

***

Love may be lost
or ventured in vain,
but whatever the cost,
we pay it in pian.

***

O Tom! I must have
 loved you too much,
for my God is a jealous God,
and acted such.

***

Boys will be boys
and girls, girls,
but nothing more annoys
than a miss too cute
for her curls.

***

If beauty be the soul of wit,
I'll try to be brief,
telling my tale
in bite-sized bits
for the logic of the plot,
and the lilt of the levity.

***

If God made the Lamb,
as Blake surmised,
and the Tyger to tear out its throat,
it's a woeful world we're in,
saints and sinners and pity
be damned.

***

The reason roses are red
and only occasionally yellow
is a question God alone
can answer, who seasoned
His world with Heaven's hues –
if He happens to be feeling mellow.

***

We live our lives
for profit and loss:
buy love with love,
giving no quarter:
the rest is dross.

***

Love may be lost
or ventured in vain,
but whatever the cost,
we pay it in pain.

WALMART A-Lot

There is something surreal
about the *Walmart,* perched
on the late-day pavement,
the letters of its calling-card,
a bloated alabaster alphabet
touting is timely merchandizing
arrival to anyone friendless
enough to be caught walking
this arid lot for autos
and restless pedestrians,
but wait, look up and gaze
amazed at the sunset sky
above the clutter of cars,
where a crimson mist is adrift
on its own motionless ocean
of air, and whatever we do
with our brick-and-mortar schemes,
there will always be beauty –
to startle, and heal.

Bemused

For Shirley McCord in fond memory

I might've been ten when Shirley
and I first noticed a pair
of dogs 'doing it' on the walk,
the doing one in a quick-witted
dither, bug-eyed and breathless,
while the object of his intentions
was a piebald pug, whose squint-
squeezed lids and lolly-
gagging tongue bespoke
her blissful acquiescence,
while Shirley looked on with bemused
scrutiny, wondering perhaps
about the size of a male's working
apparatus, and whether it'd fit.

Midnight Musing

A midnight musing: Jo-Anne
in the Hendries' henhouse,
showing off her gender's jewel,
pouting in the tender junction
of her thighs like a freckle-frenzied
friend, and I am pleased
to see that I've been blessed
with an outsize, functioning pecker,
enthused enough to puncture
a pout.

Buddy

For Alvin Gehl in fond memory

O how you chuckled whenever
I played Buddy crooning
"My Buddy" or waxing ecstatic
about the charms of Linda
or wedding-day waltzes,
knowing, as you did, that Clark
had long been eclipsed by Bing
and Perry, and bemused that such
musical schmaltz could light
my fuse.

Anchor

For Tom in fond memory

Ah, Tom, you might've mentioned
you were thinking of going – to a place
where the demons of drink aren't welcome
and the pain of their infinite itch
is soothed by the swoop of angels'
wings, for we could've had one
last colloquy about the
illimitable logic of love,
or those summers on Cameron's
blue doing when our souls
succumbed to the sun and settled
in their twinned grooves, or that
perfect poem you kept
in the word-breeding ease
of your mind till it was ready
to ripen, or the days when you toddled
in my tow like a young Apollo,
looking for a god – and I
would say thanks for the life
you anchored in mine, and wish you
well on your way out.

Duty

Whenever we boys would wade
waist-deep in Huron's
chilled fathom, the business
end of our manly rig
wizened, until it was no bigger
than a celery stalk at a ladies'
Sunday brunch or a cropped
carrot, and our testicles, in shock,
retreated to the nearest neighbourly
nook, but even then
before we were hip to the joyous
ploys of our equipment, we were certain,
without a hem or a haw
or a tinker's toot, that
when called to perform, it would thaw,
salute and do its duty.

Bath-House Blue

Whenever we compared our boys'
shy erections in the bath-house,
we called them our 'boners,'
'stiffies' or 'hard-ons,' as if
'penis' or 'prick' were too polite
an appellation for such a bodily
blooming protrusion, that a little
whittling might bring its nectar
bubbling up in joyous
profusion and wicked bedight.

Kid-Bitten

That summer when the sun
grew sulky, and we whiled
away the louring hours
in Hendrie's henhouse,
playing 'Show me yours
and mine may shine,' young
enough still to find
the erotic 'naughty,' but summers
succumb to autumn and all,
and never again would we feel
the pleasurable pinch of such
a kid-bitten innocence.

Pun-Numb

For Colm O'Sullivan in fond memory

You negotiated the pun-numbing
thickets of *Finnegans Wake!*
like an Old Irish scribe
at home in high Gaelic
or bog-brogue, just
because you could, an Erse-
versed scholar at ease
in semestered seasons, a 'Mick'
who said his prayers to any god
who could hit a two-iron
or flutter a three-foot putt,
and I see you still, a shambling,
ambling, full-rigged
figure of gratuitous girth,
combing the rough-toughened
edges for delinquent balls
or a fellow-traveller in need of a
nurturing nod, a mirthful
soul with a florid, beguiling
'begorrah' in the Celtic welter
                    of his smile.

Newborn

For Anne in fond memory

If I were one of the good
gods controlling the cosmos,
I'd enshrine you as a star in a
far-flung, filigreed
curve of the firmament or as a
moon, lit by its own
self-rinsing glow, but I am
just a word-starved bard
who has not lustre enough
to limn your loveliness or beatify
your beauty, but wherever you be,
in the star-fractured dark
or harbouring the newborn
illume of a moon, I'll send you
my love and embark on the next
body-bruising cruise
to your inner-galactic grotto
and make you mine again.

Knee-Socks & Frocks

O the gorgeous girls of the Point!
in their knee-socks and frocks,
as bright as butterflies brushed
lovely by the breeze, their black
patents toe-tapping
to the tune that hums in their heads,
their curls of every heavenly
hue: autumn-blond,
sloe aglow, rustic
red – their eyes alight
with the life blooming inside,
and O how we, bone-
bloated, thumb-clumsy,
envy the way their flue-
forged bodies dance
as if every day was a dawning –
with applause enough to bring
the joint down.

Anointed

O the girls of the Point!
with their long-legged gait,
their antelopian lope,
unimpeded by frocks
at the knees or a misbehaving
breeze that tickles their fancy
and jiggles their rig, and they seem
so much at home in their gender's
bones, in the effortless ease
of their speed that it's hard to believe
they'd soon succumb to other
hungers, other less loving
anointments.

Disarmed

For Alvin Gehl in fond memory

Whenever your mischievous mind
unbottled a naughty thought,
and you passed it along to me
with your lopsided, disarming
grin, your eyes widened like Sunday
saucers, and you paused long enough,
hedging your bets, to see
whether the wicked wit of it
had pierced my overly-educated
middle-class armour.

The Gaze

Point Edward: 1947

Edward Street School
had abutting, cindered playgrounds
to keep the genders from offending,
and when the weather was warm
and arousing, the girls, on the opposite
quad flaunted their frilly-new
frocks that left a lot
of leg and knobbly knee
to be admired and otherwise
deployed to prance, dance,
do Double-Dutch
or run till the muscles numbed,
and at any given moment,
that clioistering crew was a seething
seas of girly gams
and feminine stems that left
the ogling, yodelling boys
famished for words of praise
or approval, and loudly espousing
the rights of males to gaze
and occupy.

Where it Matters

Or roistering in the cloister

The girls we gave the nod to
were all giggles and sidelong
glances with lashes they batted
like bashful madonnas or coy
coquettes whenever we threatened
to boycott their sunny nunnery,
and we watched them from afar
like star-gazing newts
too naïve to notice the buzz
they stirred inside us, as if
some frolicsome god
had kicked us where it mattered
and smiled at our shy reply.

Brother

For Bob in loving memory

I hadn't yet learned
what "queer" meant when it wasn't
just "odd" or "funny," but I sensed
there was something like that
about your blood-and-bones
body: you weren't a roustabout
boy like the ones I bothered
to befriend, giggling with the girls
next door when a good
cuddle would've better done,
and when at last I understood
what a "fairy" was (besides
a gossamer-gal with wings),
it was too late to pretend
I wasn't chagrined by your mischievous
difference, or forgive myself
for wishing you otherwise.

Breathless

For Anne in fond memory

When I have reached my God-
allotted days, I'll save
my dying breath to blow you
the poem I've been penning
since the time I first lay
my loving eyes on yours,
not a sonnet, whose rhyme-
encrusted quatrains could not
encompass the beauty you bore
with such a winning grace,
nor a brave-heart ballad
that might catch something
of our stirring story but not
enough, and though I've composed
a dozen beguiling odes
to the way you let your eyes
do the smiling, I find that,
in the end, only an epic
would suffice with room to limn
your loveliness, but then, when God
has called my body home,
I'll have no need of words,
or thought, or breath to blow you
a perfect poem.

Three for H. D.

Petard

My pen sits poised
in its proper socket,
I wait for something
to begin within
and when it does
a weave of my words
purloins the page
and nuzzles above it,
once again I'm pleased
to be hoist on my own
bardic petard.

Undoing

This robin, freeloading
on my lawn, has the patience
of a haloed saint, head
cocked, lopsided, to catch
the thinnest throb the dew-
worm makes in his undoing.

Tufted

Somewhere aloft, a tufted
titmouse sings his *pee-ter*
pee-ter, pe-e ter, a wee
grey-backed songster
(some say blue), its breast,
wimple-white with a ruff
of rust to give it style,
sun-lit, perhaps, in the soft
simmer of the morning,
and unbeguiled by my presence,
lets his piccolo notes
grow sweeter.

Tepid

Bill Barr's *Smoke Shop*
offered us bottled Pepsi
from a cooler that hadn't seen ice
since the last glacier gave up,
but Butch and I pooled
our pennies anyway, and sipped
a single, tepid pop
with two tired straws,
and we could hear the clack
and thwack of billiard balls
and a punter's unrehearsed
curse behind the beige
curtain where no-one under
the voting age was welcomed,
and we wondered what taboo
the contraband comics, tucked
under the counter with the boot-
leg Havanas, must've broken
to warant such furtive finagling,
but by the time our best
guesses about the mechanics
of sex and its enabling apparatus
were done, so was our tepid
Pepsi.

That Day

May 8, 1945

At mid-morning on that day,
we were released from school and scrutiny
to carry the good news
abroad, and I recall 'flying'
home on my post-rheumatic
toes, ululating "The war
is over!" while our fire siren
wailed its welcome and car
horns honked volumes
and church bells clanged
with more elan than the opening
salvo at Armageddon,
and ordinary folks, like churchless
urchins, took to the streets,
where perfect strangers hugged
hugely and girls, pretty
or not, were lip-kissed,
as if it were New Year's Eve
in Kingdom Come, and I knew
that something momentous (other
than death and taxes) had happened
to the world, that the Earth had moved
another intimate inch
on its axis.

Chutzpah

For Bob in fond memory

My brother, much bolder
than I, and in the know,
sweet-talks the gamin
next door into dropping
her drawers in exchange for a
peek at his inkling dink,
and I am agog at such
chutzpah and at the petall'd
pink pout and tufted
fluff of her girly regalia,
and I read the gleam in her eyes
that says, "I know what this
is about: boys who dream
of doffing my togs and plucking
my prize.'

Just Because

With a nod to e.e.

O the girls of the Point!
in their frilly frocks, looking
like fence-flung hollyhocks
in fulsome bloom, dancing
in dithyrambic dither
in their black patents, just
because it was Just-Spring
and the world was puddle-
wonderful, and no balloon
Man whistled to the tune
that went "whee" in the loins
and settled happily there,
making worm-woo
to the apple of its eye.

God's Toddler

For Tom in fond memory

Even as a toddler, your smile
could melt a misanthrope's
hardened heart, and your blue
eyes unbuttoned the woe-
begotten world and made it
bend to Beauty and the Good,
for there was ever something
inside you that chose kindness
whenever it could and love
when nothing else would do,
and I wanted so much for you
to pass the genius in your genes
along to the generations yet
to come, where they would strut
their stuff, seethe sweetly
and induce a dozen cousin
toddlers with God's button-
blue gaze..

Slithery

Point Edward: circa 1946
My Gran lets me tag along
with her to Kopp's Meat
Market, where the tang of freshly
flayed meat hangs
in the air, and I gaze in awe
at the chops and cutlets that lie
exposed in the glassed display,
beside a shiver of liver
and a standing rib that would've
fed the multitudes
Jesus blessed with loaves
and fishes, and Butch's dad
emerges from the freezer, lugging
a half-carcass of beef
as bulked as a gutted buffalo,
and plopping it down on the big
butcher's block, awaiting
the whirr of the electric blade,
and wraps a puddle of giblets
in brown paper, ties
it tight with string from some
endless spool in the ceiling,
glances at me, and winks,
and on our way home,
something wet and slithery
drips on our shoes,
and I am thinking: someone's
got blood on their hands.

Not like This

Chatham, Ontario:
early October 1953

I must've just turned sixteen
with all my hormones humming
when I was asked to chauffeur home
a woman too drunk to tell
liquor from licorice, and someone
from my parents' party poured her
onto the seat beside me,
where she promptly passed gas,
and fell asleep, her double-chins
beginning where they began,
and all seemed well enough
until, parked below her porch,
I felt something slithery
fingering my crotch in both
directions, and I thought of the nights
I spent alone in the dark,
coaxing myself erect
and wondering what fecund flesh
might one day appease my passion;
but here and now? Not like this,
without love or the bliss it brings
to lust.

La Femme Innocente

With a nod to E.E.

O the seraphic lasses of the Point!
how they rock my octo-
generian gentility:
with those ferocious frocks
of buttercup yellow,
blues the sky would die for,
reds too hectic for the blood,
their skirts upended by the
tongue-teasing breeze
to show us a tincture of thigh
and a pair of knobbled knees,
the haloes of their hair brushed
lovely by little eddies of air,
and they seem happy to dance
their day away, pleased
to be just themselves as they be:
locked in their own precisely-
gendered trance.

Unbuckled

O the gorgeous girls of the Point!
in their fanciful frocks, ever
on the move, as if the going
was better than the getting-there,
their skirts awhirl in the flesh-
whetting wind, as if
hop-skipping a sidewalk
were the only way to travel
true, their knee-socks puddling
on their patents as they go,
and when they bend to tuck
them up, a patch of panty
winks to the boys, a-leer in the loges,
and the glance we are granted dances
our doodads, and something
in the loin comes unbuckled.

It Must be Spring

With a nod to E.E.

It must be Spring
because the ones with the curls
are giggling a jig
and doubling Dutch,
and it must be Spring
because the ones without
are rough and tumbling
and swatting a ball
too much like the moon
and it must be Spring
because the girls are frantic
with the dithering of dance
and it must be Spring
because the boys are poised
on the cusp of whatever
and somewhere off
where children can't
the Pied Piper pipes
his rueful tune
of summers come and gone
and Springs that mustn't be
and boys and girls of one begot
follow him down to Hamelin's
edge, and drown.

Twill

O the girls of the Point!
I see them still in their twilled
frocks and long-legged
stockings as white as a
novice nun's wimple,
their locks brushed akimbo
by the hot breath of the breeze,
their cheeks dimpled pink
in the telling swell of their smile,
and they are jump-skipping
to a hum in the head that teases
like a tintinnabular tantrum,
and we watch them at hopscotch
and Double Dutch, amazed,
that such creatures with nothing
notable in the crotch could dazzle,
and leave us, boy-anointed,
longing to be something other

Songtress

For Kate Smith in memoriam

Ever conscious of your girth
and those chins that wobbled
with song, you nonetheless
strode upon the stage
like a dowager queen her dais,
begowned and glowing, even though
it was only radio: you wanted
your voice to carry the image
of a home-grown songstress
to the far corners of the land you loved
and blessed with your soaring *oratundo,*
with the melodious mirth of your music,
and I see you still: in your age,
at centre ice, gowned
again, spot-lit in a beam
of admiring light, and I listen
once more as you reach again
for the final improbable note
of Berlin's anthem to America,
and hit it.

.

Elvis

There was always something a bit
raunchy about the too-smoothed
up-sweep of your locks,
or in the perpetual pout
you practiced before the mirror
each morning, or in the swivel
of your denim-zipped hips,
though you did not croon like Pat,
in love with his looks and the velvet
vim of his voice, but you sang
as if Boone and Bing had never
been, as if you knew
that *we* would be waiting in our young,
untested bones for someone
like you to tell our story,
frighten our parents and make
the break between the generations
a clean, clinical cut,
and I still recall the day
you left us, now forty and fat,
your wandering paunch, wrapped
in a sequined suit, haunted
perhaps by the thought of all
the songs you'd never sing.

Don Gutteridge
September 30, 1937 – December 01, 2023

Don, known as the **Prince of Canadian Poetry**, was born in Sarnia, Ontario and raised in the nearby village of Point Edward. He taught High School English for seven years, later becoming a Professor in the Faculty of Education at Western University, where he is now Professor Emeritus. He has published seventy-six individual books and several anthologies of selected works, including poetry, fiction and scholarly essays in literary criticism and pedagogical theory and practice.

He had published twenty-two novels, including the twelve-volume Marc Edwards mystery series and a YA fable, *The Perilous Journey of Gavin the Great*, and forty-three books of poetry, one of which, *Coppermine*, was short-listed for the 1973 Governor-General's Award. In 1970 he won the UWO President's Medal for the best periodical poem of that year, "Death at Quebec."

His poetry has been translated into Spanish by Professor Miguel Iglesias, into Chinese by Anna Yin, into Bengali by Dr. Shireen Huq and into Hindi by Dr. Giti Tyagi. Don passed on quietly in London, Ontario where he continued to write every day to his last days.

dongutteridgeauthor.ca

Bio picture by A.T. Balsara

105